Stems

by Grace Hansen

PLANT ANATOMY

Abdo
Kids

abdopublishing.com

Published by Abdo Kids, a division of ABDO, PO Box 398166, Minneapolis, Minnesota 55439.

Printed in the United States of America, North Mankato, Minnesota.

102015

012016

THIS BOOK CONTAINS
RECYCLED MATERIALS

Photo Credits: iStock, Shutterstock

Production Contributors: Teddy Borth, Jennie Forsberg, Grace Hansen

Design Contributors: Laura Mitchell, Dorothy Toth

Library of Congress Control Number: 2015942108

Cataloging-in-Publication Data

Hansen, Grace.

  Stems / Grace Hansen.

   p. cm. -- (Plant anatomy)

ISBN 978-1-68080-140-8 (lib. bdg.)

Includes index.

1. Stems (Botany)--Juvenile literature.   I. Title.

575.4--dc23

                    2015942108

Table of Contents

Stems

Stems are parts of plants. There are two main types of stems. There are **woody** stems. And there are **herbaceous** stems.

4

woody

herbaceous

5

Woody stems are covered in bark. Trees and bushes have woody stems.

Herbaceous stems are green.
They are not as strong as
woody stems. The stem
of a flower is one example.

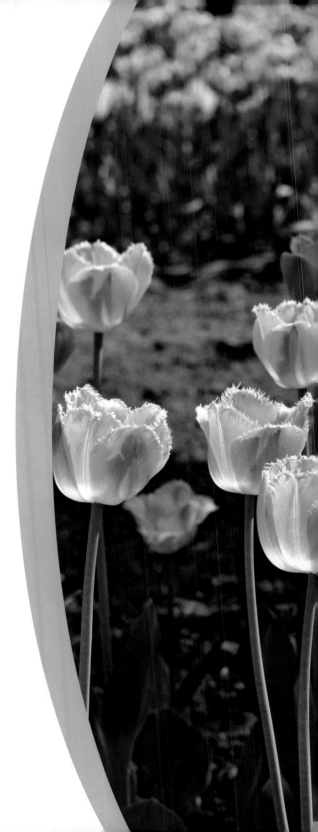

A cactus can have either type of stem. A cactus's stem is **hollow**. It stores water.

Stem Jobs

Stems are important. Stems store food. They also feed plants. They pull **nutrients** from roots.

Leaves grow from stems.

Stems keep leaves upright.

This is so they can find light.

Plants need light to grow
and make food. Stems give
some of this food to soil.
This makes soil **rich**.

Flowers grow from stems.
Stems keep flowers upright,
too. Insects can easily spot
flowers. They land on flowers
to eat **nectar**.

19

Some stems have thorns.

Thorns protect plants. No

animal wants to eat them!

Stem Types

herbaceous stem

mint

parsley

tulips

woody stem

apple tree

forsythia shrub

pine tree

22

Glossary

herbaceous (stem) – a stem that is green and bendable; flowers and herbs usually have this stem.

hollow – empty inside.

nectar – the sweet food made by a plant that attracts insects.

nutrient – something that gives nourishment for growth and health.

rich – high in plant nutrients.

woody (stem) – a stem that is hard and usually covered in bark; trees and shrubs have this stem.

Index

abdokids.com

Use this code to log on to abdokids.com and access crafts, games, videos, and more!

Abdo Kids Code:
PSK1408

DATE DUE

			PRINTED IN U.S.A.